To Pam
Love & blessings

Denni Cl
*

Crop Circle Wisdom

Crop Circle Wisdom

Simple Teachings
from the
CircleMakers

Denni Clarke

SpiritPassage
Publishing & Communications
Santa Fe, New Mexico

Published by: **SpiritPassage Publishing & Communications**
50 Agua Viviendo
Santa Fe, NM 87505

Photography: Denni Clarke
Editor: Linda Day-Schmal
Design & typography: Richard Harris

Printed in Hong Kong

ISBN: 1-929341-05-9

LLC: 00-110022

This book is dedicated to
my dear parents,
Ken and Esme Clarke

Thank you for everything

IN GRATITUDE

I would also like to thank all the beautiful beings who have helped make this journey possible:

All the people who believed in me when I didn't even believe in myself;

My family, friends, soul sisters, and star brothers, (too numerous to mention by name, but you know who you are), my beloved pets, and Everyone who has touched my life. Thank you all for your love, patience, support, and encouragement on this amazing adventure.

My Angels, Guides, and Master helpers from the Spirit world, and My Spiritual teachers from this world who have been in many forms.

And last, but not least, The CircleMakers, without whom this would not be possible.

CHERHILL, NR. CALNE, WILTSHIRE — JULY 17, 1999

Dear Reader,

This book is exactly as the title suggests – simple teachings from the CircleMakers.

I was guided by Spirit to bring back the bare, basic messages behind the pictograms, and to present them in their simplest form. I had been moved to record this information very early on in my Crop Circle experiences, but it wasn't until I was asked to speak about the sacred power of the Crop Circles, that this book started to come into being.

I was a bit worried that it was too simple at first, and I doubted myself through the process, as well. But as I continued working, I kept getting the message that this little book was actually going to do everyone a favor by bringing some real simplicity back into their lives, since life itself, these days, is overwhelmingly complicated for most people.

Like many other projects, finishing this book became a constant ongoing aim, unable to come to completion mainly because the Crop Circles are such an ongoing event – especially in my life – and due to the fact that I am a bit of a procrastinator. As my life became completely encompassed by the phenomenon, I realized more and more that I needed to wrap this

Detail, All Cannings Star – August 8, 2000

little bundle up, and get it out in some shape or form for others to experience.

So, here it is – my gift, from and to, the CircleMakers. We have been intimately interacting for six years, now. And much longer on a less conscious level.

I hope that when you pick up this little book, you are able to find a small gem of wisdom somewhere contained within its pages, meant just for you. Designed to come from the heart, it is with all positive intention that this book was created. Its heart and intention is in like fashion to my own personal and original initiation into the "Realms of Circledom" given to me by the CircleMakers, and through their most precious gift – as you are about to read.

Blessings,

Denni

WOODBOROUGH HILL, NR. ALTON PRIORS, WILTSHIRE — AUGUST 13, 2000

CONTENTS

DETAIL, SILBURY KOCH SNOWFLAKE – JULY 23, 1997

Devil's Den, nr. Clatford, Wiltshire — July 19, 1999

INTRODUCTION

Welcome to the most amazing mystery of our times. There is so much that we don't know about the beautiful Crop Circles that are appearing in our fields – what they are, how they are formed, or what they mean. The more that time goes by, the more the mystery seems to deepen. They appear in greater complexity and abundance, over more distances, and still the awesome wonder of them is the only thing we can be sure of. We do know, however, that they are most unique, and create a place of special distinction – even sacredness.

The circle is the most ancient and basic of Sacred symbols, used for centuries as a way of creating a vortex and for focusing energy, and it seems appropriate to term these newer, precious circles as modern-day Sacred sites. Since the ancient Sacred sites, to which the CircleMakers seem to be drawn, were known to be gateways for interdimensional travel, it stands to reason that maybe these newer sites could also have the same possibilities.

The incredible multi-facetted, multi-layered Crop Circle phenomenon, with its intricate precision of design and form, presents gifts of beauty to our visual senses. It also connects us to a deeper sense of ourselves, our relationship to each other, and to the Earth and the Universe – and to an awareness of our Universal interconnectedness as we awaken to the knowledge of our Greater Reality, like a transcendental mystery.

INTERIOR, WINDMILL HILL TRIPLE JULIA, NR. AVEBURY, WILTSHIRE — JULY 29, 1996

The Crop Circles certainly do have the ability to change lives, and are truly transformational. And if we are open to it, they invite us to participate in a huge consciousness leap. They also allow us to access truth and knowledge on whatever level we are capable of.

However you look at it, the CircleMakers offer us a multitude of opportunities for personal growth, consciousness exploration, and help with our spiritual evolution during our physical experiences here on Earth. It is with acceptance of this caring offer, in the form of Love and Light, that this book is written.

PEWSEY WHITE HORSE FORMATION — AUGUST 7, 2000

The
CIRCLEMAKER'S
GIFT

A True Story

Once upon a time, after a great shaking of the Earth, one – amongst many – of the planetary Light Workers awoke from a deep sleep in the "illusion."

She had awoken before, but not like this. The dreams ended, and she was able to see, hear, and feel more fully – in more totality. The awakening shifted her consciousness like the dawning of a new day that was brighter and more blessed than even the most special day of her previous life. It made her most aware that the truth about the inner calling that had drawn her to travel to the new land was about to be revealed in some way.

An innocent, she was, and she had many lessons to learn. She embarked on an adventure of reconnection to her home-land, not really knowing where she was going, or where it would eventually lead her, but realizing it was an important journey. Many times she almost gave up. And she prayed for someone to come and help her, not realizing, at first, that she had much help in unseen forms, and that she had to experience all the hardships on the journey so that she could grow and fully

Detail, All Cannings Star – August 8, 2000

experience the pleasure of the free flowing grace when it was time. As the years went by, and she grew stronger and more comfortable in her new role, more magic started occurring in her life.

She followed the call of Spirit, and found that the more she acknowledged and trusted where it took her, the more that her life was embraced by this so-called magic. Love surrounded her, and the energy of loving beings supported her, and she realized that this love was the essence of All That Is.

As she shed her layers of fear and conditioning, and scars of the past, and broke through to the truth of her mission here on Earth, she received "the gift" – a small, but most precious present in the form of a personal Crop Circle in the wild grasses of the old overgrown orchard outside her home.

What greater personal acknowledgement could have been bestowed upon her! She knew she had been truly blessed.

BISHOP'S CANNINGS – JUNE 27, 2000

SETTING THE SCENE

Firstband Experience

Since it was mentioned that my experiences inspired me to write this book, I'd like to offer a few of them here to create a background of Crop Circle country – especially for those of you who haven't had the opportunity to experience the Crop Circles firsthand.

There are so many pictures that come to mind at first, incorporating sight, sound, smell, and feelings, that it's hard to know where to start. It is an awesome sight – catching sight of a crop formation in a field as one is driving along a country lane. The average size of these formations is probably 250 ft. in diameter, and many are much larger than that.

I remember the thrill of spotting my first Crop Circle as I was on the road towards Glastonbury. I had taken a route that was very familiar to me. Not actually having intended to go that way, my automatic pilot guided me on. Before I knew it, I was on the A4 towards Avebury, the heart of Crop Circle country. It was a simple circle in the field opposite Silbury Hill, the centre of many cosmic experiences for a lot of us.

Another synchronicity on this same trip, was the occurrence of two Crop Circles in the Midlands where my parents

GROUND SHOT OF LIDDINGTON CASTLE CRESCENTS – AUGUST 2, 1996

lived. The two Crop Circles appeared in the same field – one a simple circle, the other a circle with an outer ring – on the farmland that was very familiar to me. I had played in those very fields as a child, and still enjoyed walking the footpath through them when visiting. They had appeared on the very same day that my plane had landed on my journey from San Francisco to London Heathrow!

The third and most profound of all my experiences on this particular journey was the first time I actually set foot inside of a Crop Circle. I was with a larger group of people who had all come from the Crop Circle Symposium in Glastonbury. I remember the excitement and anticipation I felt as we neared the field, and could vaguely spot the outline of the formation in the waving ears of wheat. It was the Roundway formation of 1995, near Devizes in Wiltshire – two separate circles – one small centre circle, and another larger circle, both surrounded by an outer ring that kissed the outer edge of the larger circle. Again, it was a simple formation; one that had actually been laid a couple of weeks prior, and had been quite well visited already.

Were the CircleMakers trying to tell me something about simplicity at the very beginning, as I gazed at my very first Crop Circle from within its midst? Did not this indicate that simplicity, time, and the amount of visitors to a formation are irrelevant to the experiences that one can glean from it?

I'll never forget the feeling I got as I stepped through the

INTERIOR, BECKHAMPTON STAR, NR. AVEBURY, WILTSHIRE — AUGUST 8, 1998

"gateway" from the tramlines into the outer ring, right by the intersection of the larger circle. There was a rush of energy that came up from the Earth through my body; while simultaneously, a cosmic energy entered my crown chakra from above, both seeming to activate the opening and aligning of my chakras concurrently. As they met – right in my heart chakra – I experienced an intense emotion of love, joy, and well being like I have never experienced before – a true heart–opening feeling. It was then that I realized that the energies behind these incredible Crop Circles were very benevolent and highly spiritually evolved.

I call this my "initiation," as it changed my life forever, and has enabled me to connect with this energy almost at will, expand my awareness, and embark on adventures I'd never dreamed of. During all my years of visiting the Crop Circles, I have never had this experience duplicated, although almost two years later, I did have a very similar experience when I was actually visited by the CircleMakers in California when they left me my "personal gift." And at this time, it was interesting to observe my own reactions, which initially were ones of momentary disbelief, and then as if entering some kind of altered state that isolated me from rational thinking (like taking a photo to record it). Since it was in green wild oats, it wasn't long before the spring's warm sunshine would encourage the unharmed bent stalks to stand tall once more. I was completely awestruck, that time! It was another profound message for me, but so per-

Ground shot of Liddington Castle Fractal – August 2, 1996

sonal and private that I had to process the extremity of it all before I could even talk about it. It all had to do with the changes in my life, that at the time, needed to take place, and that had finally come about to enable me to clear the pathway to move on, and move forward.

But, back to England –

The first thing one is aware of in Crop Circle country is the overall pleasant feeling one gets from being there. Visually, the lush green and golden fields, the gentle, rolling hills, and the contented animals grazing in meadows give the feeling of a pastoral peacefulness of days gone by, when life moved at a much slower pace. In fact, we can truly immerse ourselves in this setting as we meander around the country lanes in search of the precious Circles. And we can continue this same feeling; whether it be visiting the formations in the early morning with the dew's crystal droplets shining brightly on standing stalks; or the heavy warmth of the midday sunshine emitting a stillness over the land; or the magic of an evening sunset coloring the skies. Taking time to sit, stand, or tread softly through the fields in silence, one becomes so much more aware of all the wonderful gifts of Nature, and the subtle differences between each moment in time – like the smell of the dampness of dawn compared to the warmth of the wheat under the sun; or indeed, the early summer's aliveness compared to the laid back feeling that occurs later on.

Silbury Hill, nr. Avebury, Wiltshire — July 24, 2000

Of course, all of these experiences are very healing to one's whole being, as are most of the feelings one gets from being inside of the formations, themselves. Whether it is from sitting, quietly meditating alone or in a larger group, or sharing experiences with others in the Circles, a sense of contentment comes over you. The Circles are such wonderful meeting places where many a friendship has been struck with a complete stranger, or been rekindled with a friend seldom seen.

In this magical domain, even when one is by one's self, there is the distinct feeling of never being alone. I personally have never found it to be uncomfortable in any way. Maybe my own belief that an Angelic presence is with me at all times has a lot to do with it, as I have called upon their assistance on many occasions to help me find hard to reach formations. I do know, however, that there seems to be a guiding Light behind all this wonderful weirdness. And I hope that those who have not, and maybe do not, get a chance to join those of us fortunate enough to immerse ourselves in these fields of mystery each year, will at least be touched in some way by the messages and photographs presented in this book, that share the mystery and magic The Circles bring to us.

PICKED HILL, NR. ALTON BARNES, WILTSHIRE – JULY 15, 2000

"The world will never starve for want of wonders; but only for want of wonder."

G.K. Chesterton

ACCEPTANCE

Acceptance is the first precept that the CircleMakers teach us, for without acceptance of these beautiful manifestations, we cannot even appreciate the gifts that are being offered us, let alone explore deeper.

Yet sometimes, even from just viewing the images, there is such a shift on a cellular level, that the acceptance of them can happen in a very subtle and gentle way. We realize that we are not in control, that there is some greater force at work in the Universe.

One of the hardest things for some people to come to terms with is the acceptance of something that is out of their range of understanding and that they have no control over. When we accept this, we can truly learn to flow; we can tap into this energy that they bring us. That is when the synchronicities and the magic start to take place. When we can accept, and let go of old and outdated belief patterns, it creates a space for expansion within us.

INTERIOR, BISHOPS CANNINGS, WILTSHIRE – JUNE 27, 2000

"The real voyage of discovery consists not in seeking new landscapes,
but in having new eyes."

Marcel Proust

APPRECIATION

Through appreciation of these patterns in the fields, we can truly come to treasure life and the simple, basic things about it that we sometimes take for granted.

It is so important to not take anything for granted, especially today, when everything is changing, and the changes are happening so rapidly. Appreciate and enjoy every moment; each one is very precious. Appreciate yourself and everyone you meet. Treat every being with kindness.

Appreciate Mother Earth and all the life she sustains, and the beauty of her glory in all its diversity. Appreciate the fresh air we breathe, and the waters that support life. Appreciate the food as it grows in the field, and those who tend it carefully to bring it to our table.

Appreciate the simple pleasures of the countryside – the peacefulness, the wildflowers by the wayside, the birdsong in the hedgerows, the trees in their many varieties and forms.

Appreciate the company of others as we learn to commune gently, and flow with the seasons – all of which the CircleMakers have us pay attention to as we anticipate, and then enjoy, the splendor of their artwork. Maybe we don't need to figure them out; maybe we just need to embrace their wonder, and enjoy them as a part of the Great Mystery.

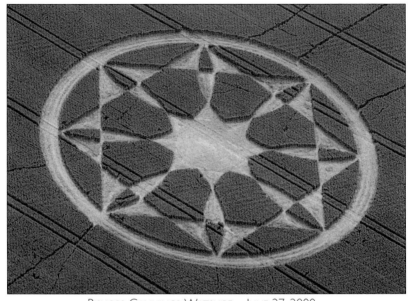

BISHOPS CANNINGS, WILTSHIRE – JUNE 27, 2000

"*Though we travel the world over to find the beautiful, we must carry it with us or we find it not.*"

Ralph Waldo Emerson

BEAUTY

Beauty – their exquisite beauty – is the first quality we are struck by when we come upon the Crop Circles.

Their magnificent artwork is something that we can't deny. Whoever is behind all of these has to be some kind of incredible artist. And to incorporate the extraordinary display of Sacred Geometry into the images, and to give us all the tender detailing that is only seen and appreciated on the ground from inside the formations, that's impressive!

Once we acknowledge this beauty, we seem to become more conscious of all the other beauty around us in each living thing – even in ourselves and in each other – and the inner beauty of each spirit, and the threads of life force that create the great tapestry when woven together. This will truly help us to walk the path of beauty, and to honor it in our daily lives, in as many ways as we can, starting from within.

Let it shine forth, and spread out into the world, touching every being, and linking Light in as many ways as possible, transforming the world into a place we have only imagined in our dreams.

UFFINGTON WHITE HORSE NR. WOOLSTONE, OXFORDSHIRE – JULY 22, 2000

"Still round the corner there may wait, a new road or a secret gate."
J.R.R. Tolkein

FLEXIBILITY

The CircleMakers have a wonderful way of teaching us how to be flexible.

Whether it be the number of times that plans have been changed because there is some incredible new formation to go and visit, or you bump into a friend you haven't seen for a year when you had plans to be elsewhere, you will notice, how even in your own lives these days, more and more plans change hourly. It is the Universe trying to get the message to us to "be" in the moment – to follow Spirit without hesitation, which is not always as easy as it sounds.

But once started in small ways, it has a way of becoming easier. And pretty soon, one can get into a flow, and learn how to incorporate spontaneity into one's life without being totally irresponsible. Once this flexibility is mastered, synchronicities abound. The easiest way to get started is to have no expectations, or to "expect the unexpected."

It is important, in these times, to be able to achieve as much flexibility as possible. Because as things move faster and faster, we are then able to adapt to choosing the path of Highest Good for our own being, as the changes occur.

INTERIOR (WITH LIGHT ANOMALIES), DEVIL'S DEN, NR. CLATFORD, WILTSHIRE
JULY 19, 1999

"Nothing is more honorable than a grateful heart."

Seneca

GRATITUDE

One of the greatest teachings of the CircleMakers is that of gratitude – gratitude for life itself, and the opportunity for the expansive and heart–opening experiences that come along with the exploration of these amazing mysteries.

Even gratitude for the challenges that present themselves along the way is taught to us. When we can be grateful for everything, we notice that we have blessings beyond belief. We realize the incredible space it enables us to enter.

The more one gives thanks, the more one has to be thankful for. And along with gratitude, is taking nothing for granted. For, once something is taken for granted, the magic of it disappears. Make it a point each day to remember the things you have to be thankful for.

Express gratitude in as many ways as possible. Say "thank you" out loud, write "thank you" on your checks, and tell others "thank you," often. Give thanks for friends and loved ones. Give thanks for everything in your life, from the roof over your head, to the food on your table, and for all the everyday things that enable you to keep going.

Even give thanks for things that look like pitfalls along your path. For when we look back in retrospect, we see that "every cloud has a silver lining," and that the little rocks we stumbled

CLEY HILL, NR. WARMINSTER, WILTSHIRE – JULY 14, 1997

over, or the mountains that we had to climb along the way, revealed something very special that would never have occurred if we hadn't traveled that route.

Father Charlie Moore, a local "emissary of Light," put it all in a nutshell, one day, when he described "grace" in a very touching way. He said that grace was "the overflowing ecstasy of gratitude." Yes, may everyone experience grace, and may the blessings be!

So, "thank you," CircleMakers, for entering into our reality, and for allowing us to experience transformation in such a delightful way.

MARTINSELL HILL, NR. CLENCH, WILTSHIRE — AUGUST 10, 2000

"The secret of life is balance, and the absence of balance is life's destruction."

Inayat Khan

HARMONY

Harmony can be learned and experienced from the gentle way in which we are approached by the CircleMakers.

We can choose to observe the phenomenon or not. We can accept it or not. We can also learn harmony from the application of the formations by the way in which the swirled designs do no harm to the actual crop, and the way in which they harmonize into the landscape. There is also a great harmony in the shapes of the patterns themselves – the geometry of them, and the precision of their application.

We also learn to harmonize with each other, and co–operate instead of creating conflict, as all our different ideas and perceptions create a rich tapestry of diversity. In recognition of this, we create balance in our lives and in our world.

We have no definitive answers to this phenomenon; it is still a great mystery. And as hard as it is for us, sometimes, not to project our ideas onto others, we must learn to respect others opinions, even when they differ so completely from our own. Just as each crop formation is totally unique and special in its own right, we must recognize that each of us is a totally unique and special being, each with one's own special gifts, personal opinions, and unique ideas.

Honoring this naturally creates more harmony in one's own life, and ultimately in the lives of others.

INTERIOR, EAST KENNETT GRID, NR. AVEBURY, WILTSHIRE — JULY 2, 2000

"The road that is built in hope is more pleasant to the traveler than the road built in despair, even though they both lead to the same destination."

Marion Zimmer Bradley

HOPE

In these times of quickening and change, it is easy to lose hope of good things for the future.

Sometimes when we look at the way the world is going, we get a bit despondent, to say the least. The prophecies point to some major cataclysmic event, or to destruction of our world as we know it. And certainly, when we look at the way life was, as we once knew it, we know it will never be that same way again.

For sure, our lovely planet is in deep trouble, with all the lack of respect and abuse it gets. The environment is polluted beyond belief. The population is expanding so rapidly that it is completely out of control, and the technology we have, in most instances, only goes further to create more havoc.

The Crop Circles, to many of us, are cosmic messages of awakening, and they do, indeed, seem to be able to touch many people on many levels with their symbology alone. The Intelligence behind these glyphs cleverly appeals to people of all cultures, all races, and all creeds, from all walks of life. They attempt to reach us in whatever way they are able, with respect for our own personal freedom and free will.

Within this awakening is the feeling of anticipation and excitement of things about to unfold. Most of us acknowledge the existence of other beings in the Universe, many of which

DETAIL, TAWSMEAD COPSE, WEST STOWELL, WILTSHIRE — AUGUST 9, 1998

truly care about our future and us. When you think about it, if we fail in our responsibilities as custodians of the Earth, we affect the whole Universe. So why shouldn't there be many who are concerned for us?

One of the hardest things for us to do is to ask for help, but that's all we have to do. There are many wise and wonderful beings ready to give us a helping hand. We just have to learn to get into the habit of asking for help.

The energies of the CircleMakers seem to be in alignment with that of the Angels, and that's what "they" love to do – to help us. But of course, only if we ask, as they respect our free will. So keep that in mind, and start to get in touch with asking for help. It creates a hopeful future, if collectively, we empower ourselves.

The feeling of being supported is very wonderful; and becomes reinforced throughout our everyday life the more we interact on these levels, and the more we start to manifest what we would really like. We are not alone.

EAST KENNETT, NR. AVEBURY, WILTSHIRE
HEART – JULY 15, 2000; GRID – JULY 2, 2000

"*Humility like darkness reveals the heavenly lights.*"

Henry David Thoreau

HUMILITY

The CircleMakers teach us to be humble, especially when one is eager for explanations.

When we have looked for mental solutions to the mystery, most so called answers have been quickly disproved by the next season.

We have all had the experience of being wrong about something, and having to face the humbling experience of having to admit it. It is a good lesson to be open. And to not be influenced by others, but to just come from the heart with how things feel. And it's also a good lesson to know it's ok to be wrong. After all, we are only human, and how can we learn if we don't make a few mistakes along the way?

The hardest lesson is learning to let go of our ego and step aside. Once we can do that, we can truly be humble.

GOLDEN BALL HILL, NR. ALTON BARNES, WILTSHIRE – JULY 17, 2000

"The snow goose need not bathe to make itself white. Neither need you
do anything but be yourself."

Lao–tse

INNOCENCE

The CircleMakers have given us the lovely gift of being able to rekindle our true sense of wonder.

With innocence comes a wonderful openness that allows Spirit to work in magical ways. The CircleMakers have a way of working with everyone according to one's capabilities. If we can approach the phenomenon with an openness and sense of innocence, we can avoid the pitfalls of dogmatism, and gain fresh perspectives with each new and wonderful formation. This doesn't mean being ignorant, for we need to approach many matters on this path with caution and discernment.

Our true sense of wonder is something that we lost, or became hidden, over the course of the last century, with all the technology, and being required to center our awareness in the brain, having to figure things out. Wonder ties in with innocence and the sense of awe that is really inspiring to our perceptions. It stimulates a high level of feeling and creative expression within us.

ALL CANNINGS, WILTSHIRE – AUGUST 8, 2000

"*Dream to touch the stars and live to touch your dreams.*"

Anonymous

Intention

Almost everyone in the field can relate an experience of their own, or from someone they know personally, who has had the precious gift of complete communion with the CircleMakers through the manifestation of a thought, wish, or positive intent, appearing in the form of a crop circle.

Indeed, we have even heard of some pranksters being converted into "croppies" by going to the field, and finding their intended pattern already in form. The whole thing makes us very aware of focusing our thoughts on the truly positive. And that for every thought, there is some kind of action. "Where the attention goes, the energy flows."

A new awareness is creeping into the population, and it is good to nurture it with gentle and positive tools such as those the CircleMakers are creating for us. They change our way of looking at things, for each person can tune into that frequency, as much or as little as they want to, and are capable of, and embark on an incredible transformational journey.

SILBURY HILL, NR. AVEBURY, WILTSHIRE
TRIPLET – JULY 6, 2000; STARS – JULY 24, 2000

"Fortune will call at the smiling gate."

Chinese Proverb

JOY

The CircleMakers allow us to enter the space of joy easily.

They, themselves, have a great sense of play in the way they teach us, with their unpredictability each season, and with what transpires during that space in time.

The joy that radiates from the people you meet inside of the Crop Circles is plain to see; and, indeed, many have been overcome by uncontrollable mirth from just the energies, alone. The laughter and the wonderful camaraderie one has with others, as stories and experiences are exchanged, bring joy out of the sharing and the opening of hearts.

This is an important lesson – not to take things too seriously. Life is supposed to be fun! We chose to be here at this exciting time. Celebrate life! Take time to play.

We have the most beautiful planet here – this very precious Earth – with such an incredible amount of diversities to enjoy and behold, and so little time in which to do it.

Lightness is the answer. Be light, and of the Light, and joy will then become a natural part of you and your life. Be joyful in the dance of life, and more joy will surround you!

GIANTS GRAVE, NR.. OARE, WILTSHIRE – AUGUST 3, 2000

"*The real voyage of discovery consists not in seeking new landscapes,
but in having new eyes.*"

Marcel Proust

LETTING GO/RELEASE

Required at both the beginning and the end of our Crop Circle experience, letting go and releasing is a paramount lesson given to us by the CircleMakers.

The first thing we have to let go of, is our preconceived ideas and existing beliefs about the phenomena, as we go deeper into our exploration of the mystery. And the last thing we have to let go of, is our attachment to the Crop Circles, themselves. With the ripening of the crop, and the eventual harvest at the end of the season, the beautiful images disappear; first of all, as the formation is cut, and then completely, as the ground is ploughed for its wintering. Much as we would love to be able to have a constant, living visual image of these precious designs, we have to eventually let go, creating space for a new opening and the next step of the journey.

An extremely important lesson at this time is the importance of releasing the things that don't serve us anymore – whether it be a job, a relationship, an idea, or a concept. Don't waste time with "what-ifs"; time is short. There is an urgency to proceed upon the journey, with as clear a path laid before us as possible, so that we can move with the energy of the moment without making too many compromises, and do what is needed to move forward. There is no longer any room for any "excess

Cherhill, nr. Calne, Wiltshire – July 17 1999

baggage." It is cumbersome and restrictive, inhibiting our progress and personal growth. So the sooner we lighten our load, the easier things get.

Let go and create an open space for more magical events to take place!

HACKPEN HILL, NR. BROAD HINTON, WILTSHIRE – JULY 4, 1999

"When you give with love, not expectation, you receive more than you ever thought possible."

Beth Mende Conny

LOVE

Love is the ultimate creative energy of the Universe. Those people sensitive and lucky enough to experience this through the Crop Circles and the cosmic/Earth/heart connection have truly received another gift from the CircleMakers.

"Love is all you need." Love is all there is! When we realize that this energy has the capability of connecting the cosmic life force energy with the Earth energy through the heart, it becomes the most heart-opening experience one can imagine.

The feeling of utmost benevolence and love energy from Source is always there. It is within us, and surrounds us, so we can access it at any time. The more we draw from it, the more connected to Source we become. As this whole energy becomes a greater part of our life, we learn to love ourselves more.

From there we can learn to love others with greater understanding and compassion, eventually learning how to love unconditionally, without feeling the need to burden ourselves with attachment to their process.

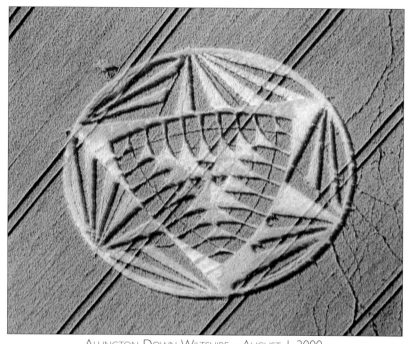

ALLINGTON DOWN, WILTSHIRE – AUGUST 1, 2000

"Judge not a man until you have walked a mile in his moccasins."

Sioux Proverb

NON-JUDGEMENT

Most Crop Circle researchers have experienced non-judgement firsthand at some time or another in the field.

We have failed to explore a particular formation because of some pre-judgement, only to discover later on, that we either delayed the joy of exquisite intricacies that were hidden from us until inside the formation, or maybe we missed out on the whole experience altogether.

And so it is in life.

This is a good one, and a hard lesson! Once our awareness has tuned into not being judgmental, we realize just how judgmental we can be! It will then come right back to hit us square in the face.

We judge ourselves; we judge each other. We put judgement on all sorts of things and situations that we have no right to be involved in, and shouldn't waste energy on. And we just end up acting as mirrors for each other, anyway.

So, let's look for the good in ourselves and each other before we start expounding on the faults. We will then end up creating more harmony in our own lives, as well as in others.

HONEY STREET, NR. ALTON BARNES, WILTSHIRE – JULY 16, 1999

"There is no peace, except the peace in a man's heart."

Anonymous

PEACE

The Crop Circles are certainly conducive to obtaining a peaceful state.

They lie patiently in the lush countryside, waiting to be discovered. And then give us the gift of peace, as we touch the Earth amongst their delicate patterning. They bring us the quiet stillness of nature herself – the songs of the birds, the feel of the wind, the warmth of the sun, the freshness of the air, the soft colors of the wildflowers in the hedgerows, and the golden waving ears of wheat. Small wonder, that so many people love to meditate within the formations.

But the peace really begins inside us in our own hearts. Once we can reach that place, it can radiate out to others, and expand and make the world a better place.

Thank you, CircleMakers, for giving us the opportunity of achieving that space more easily from within your beautiful glyphs!

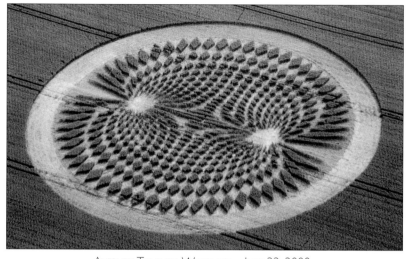

"Glory not in what you are, but in what you have the power to become."

Anonymous

POWER

The Crop Circles, encompassing the Universal language of Sacred Geometry, and containing frequencies that have the capabilities of affecting so many of us on so many levels, are definitely almighty and powerful in their application and impact.

They are truly powerful in many ways, but the tenderness with which they are brought to our attention is quite remarkable.

Normally when we use the word power, it has the connotation of something mighty and often threatening. But if we use the word "soft," (like soft-power) or place the letters "e-m" in front of it to form the word "empower," then it has a much different implication.

This is the lesson here. We can use our own power in a quiet and non-threatening way to make changes in the world – starting first with ourselves. The power of thought, intention, words, and deeds is something that the majority of people are not familiar with. Each is a vibration that has so much potential and impact on all levels as it is released into existence, that we can change the world if we truly believe it.

Let us be conscious of this, and strive to be more fully aware of what we are putting out into the Universe!

AVEBURY TRUSLOE INTERIOR – JULY 22, 2000

"No act of kindness, no matter how small, is ever wasted."

Aesop

RESPECT

The CircleMakers certainly seem to respect us and the spaces that they utilize for their artwork.

They don't push their images in front of our faces; we have to "discover" them. They also have a respect for life, since they gently lay the crop without breaking the stalks. They seem to choose sites with great respect, too; picking places according to energy fields and placement in the landscape.

In like fashion, we are taught to respect the fields in our approach to entry by walking in to the formations along the tramlines, and respecting the farmers by obtaining permission for entry beforehand. We also ask permission from Source to enter a formation, as some are not conducive to one's own personal frequency.

In reverence to the Sacred space of which the Crop Circles warrant, it makes us consciously respect the whole Earth as Sacred, also. To respect the beauty of our Earth, our resources, and especially the water and the food that nurtures us; respecting each other, and all the living things that we share our life with on this precious planet, is a gift of insight the CircleMakers have given us.

ALLINGTON DOWN, WILTSHIRE — JUNE 24, 1999

"Trust me, but look to thyself."

Irish Proverb

 TRUST

The CircleMakers manage to put us in a state of trust each year – a trust that they will return with the gifts of their images in the fields once more.

We know never to take that trust for granted. We are rewarded with their presence, and then gifted with not only the magnificent formations, but with the aliveness that encompasses the energies of being around them.

Trust is an intense concept for most people to conquer. We are so used to being in control, or thinking we are – or wanting to be. We also have many fears; many of which are programmed into our being from an early age.

We have to learn to surrender before we can completely trust. Once accomplished, the magic begins, and synchronicities abound.

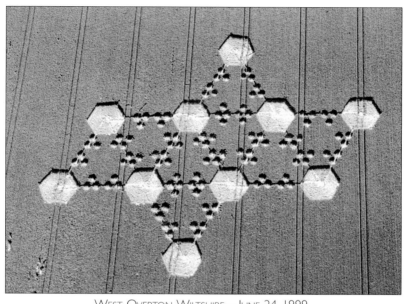

WEST OVERTON, WILTSHIRE – JUNE 24, 1999

"The truth dazzles gradually, or else the world would be blind."

Emily Dickenson

TRUTH AND INTEGRITY

As with the integrity we know is required in our own lives to create a strong foundation for our spiritual growth, so the CircleMakers teach us that this same integrity is an important part of each moment of our lives.

Once we work with these energies, we become acutely aware that if we are not existing in integrity, we will become separated from the wholeness of "All That Is." And that wholeness centers on living in our truth.

Truth and integrity go hand in hand with each other, and both are extremely important in this day and age. With the accelerated pace of life, and the instant "karma" effect, if we do not completely come from our heart, and exist in our own truth, then we will find it difficult to transcend this period of time smoothly.

Juxtaposed to truth is integrity. Integrity is one of the building blocks of a truthful life. Something, or someone, lacking in integrity is not very strong, stable, or resilient.

As the energies of the Crop Circles direct us in teaching us to center ourselves in our own heart and in our own truth, we become clear and of a clean conscience, moving forward smoothly and with ease on the path that sets before us.

WOODBOROUGH HILL, NR. ALTON PRIORS, WILTSHIRE — AUGUST 13, 2000

"Joy is the realization of oneness, the oneness of our soul with the world and of the world, and of the world-soul with the supreme love."

Rabindranath Tagore

UNITY

Unity is the ultimate message of the CircleMakers.

It is the message of the Masters from the beginning of time. It is the message of all the shamans and gurus, and spiritual teachers. It is the only real lesson that we need to learn, for once we get it, then we have it. When we can release ourselves from the illusion of separateness, and recognize our interconnectedness with all life, then we are able to truly dance the dance of "beingness," and enjoy our physicality.

As we come together to share our interest in these mysteries, let us celebrate and enjoy our lives, and acknowledge the unity that the CircleMakers so eloquently teach us. When they present us with such exquisite patterns that seem to remind us that we are all connected, we sense and know from somewhere inside our being, that what affects one, ultimately affects us all.

Let us pray that eventually the interconnectedness of all life will be a conscious aspect of all beings, and that we can enjoy this special place that we inhabit with all the special beings that we share it with, in perfect peace.

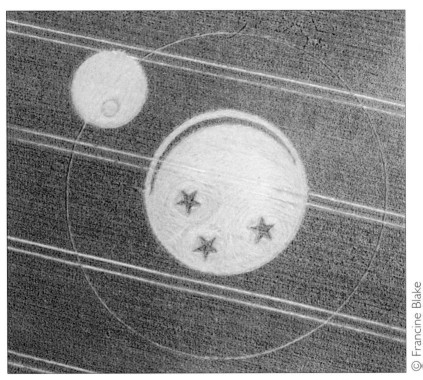

PEWSEY WHITE HORSE, PEWSEY, WILTSHIRE — AUGUST 7, 2000

"The highest wisdom is kindness."

The Talmud

WISDOM

The wisdom that is gleaned from the Crop Circles is not the kind of understanding that comes from knowledge of the mind, but of a deeper kind – through the heart.

Such wisdom is not really obtainable through words or by way of our general means of transmission. It is a kind of wisdom that comes from deep inside; gained from experiences, rather like the knowledge from the Mystery Schools and ancient esoteric teachings that haven't been tampered with by humankind.

Maybe these images were programmed into our genetic coding long ago, and we are only now remembering on a deeper level, something about their significance as we visit them again. Certainly, many people seem to recognize the images in some way, shape, or form, but have no recollection of exactly from where, or when.

This wisdom is the kind of knowing that one has, which is just a feeling that can't be put into words – like a purity of connection to Spirit.

Namasté

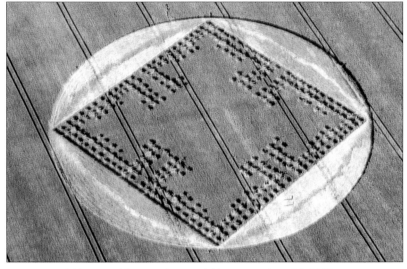

WINDMILL HILL, NR. AVEBURY, WILTSHIRE — JULY 16, 1999

So . . .
WHO ARE THESE CIRCLEMAKERS?

Since it is all such a wonderful mystery, and nobody really knows, we can only speculate on exactly who is behind this incredible phenomenon. What we do know, is that very few Crop Circles are manmade. Whatever claims are made publicly or over the Internet about hoaxes, there is never the evidence to support them.

The fact is, these patterns in the fields are appearing worldwide, and in greater numbers and complexity.* They are mostly formed at night in a matter of seconds. And there is scientific evidence that supports the fact that chemical changes actually take place within the plants inside the formations, which has most notably been investigated by Dr. Leavengood at his lab in Michigan, in the United States. The energies of the formations themselves are dowsable, and research carried out regarding recordable, electro-magnetic data is undeniable. More and more research involving harmonics is also being documented – and on and on.

––––––––––

* Grain crops are not the only medium the CircleMakers use. Patterns have been found in sand, snow, ice, salt flats, rice and even trees.

BISHOPS CANNINGS, WILTSHIRE — JULY 25, 2000

Many people feel that there is an extraterrestrial energy behind the Crop Circles. Could they be made by some non-physical beings, or beings from another dimension? Some believe that the Earth, herself, may be responsible – recognizing her as Gaia, a thinking being. And there has been speculation that Earth spirits, or devas, may have some interaction, also. Then there are those who believe Angels or Ascended Masters play a part. Could it possibly be a co-operation of all of these beings and entities; even our own selves interacting on some level of consciousness that we can't truly explain?

ALL CANNINGS, WILTSHIRE – AUGUST 7, 2000

And . . .
WHY ARE THEY HERE?

This is another part of the mystery that we can only speculate. Could it be that the Crop Circles are messages from some very highly evolved spiritual beings? Beings who care about us so deeply that they are trying desperately to awaken us all to the fact that they are very concerned about us and how we are conducting our lives on Earth? After all, there are so many in the world who have lost touch with the reality that all things are connected. And that by losing the sanctity of their connection with nature, they are creating an uninhabitable planet for future generations; if indeed, there are not those that will destroy it before then!

Maybe the CircleMakers are here to reconnect us with Spirit. Or could the Crop Circles be some kind of modern day portals or spiritual gateways to help us access higher states of consciousness just as the stone circles were? Could there also be the possibility that the Crop Circles are placed for some kind of energetic healing to bring back balance to our Earth?

Whatever their purpose, and whoever is behind their beautiful creations, we welcome them each summer.

Thank you CircleMakers.

NORTH DOWN, NR. BECKHAMPTON, WILTSHIRE — JULY 25, 2000

A CIRCLE COMPLETED –

SYNCHRONICITIES OF SPIRIT

I feel that I have to add this little extra to the book because of all the amazing synchronicities that started to take place after I had mentally committed to getting this book published. It had been sitting around for over three years. I had submitted it to several publishers, none of who felt it quite right for them, but who had given me encouragement. This left me with a feeling of hope, but I wasn't quite sure what to do next.

During that year, however, I was introduced to Linda Day-Schmal, who had a small publishing company named SpiritPassage. I really liked her, and felt very in tune with her approach to the business and its mission of working with Spirit and Higher Consciousness. Somehow this seemed so right for what the CircleMakers wanted to put out, but at that time SpiritPassage was just beginning to help people publish in paperback.

As time went by, I thought of SpiritPassage quite a lot, and one day I received an e-mail from Linda. She said that she had been thinking of me because SpiritPassage had gone through some progressive changes – all for the better – having more capabilities than before, and now was a non-profit ministry organization. She stated that a few weeks after having thought of me, and upon receiving a subscription copy of a magazine,

ROUNDWAY, DEVIZES, WILTSHIRE – JULY 31, 1999

she saw that it included an article on Crop Circles, and thought of me, again. As she gazed at the article, she then noticed that I had written the article! And it was then that she contacted me. I thought this was all very cosmic, and took it as a sign that at last I had found whom I wanted to work with.

Meanwhile, I went to visit an old friend who has always been very supportive of my endeavors, and when I mentioned to him that I was going to get my book published, he immediately offered to help fund the project. I thought this was extremely generous of him; yet I wanted him to know what he was going to be backing, so I sent him a copy of my manuscript to look over. I could hardly believe it when he called to say that he loved it, and that there would be a check arriving in the mail. Now I really knew that Spirit was working with me on this!

Though even with his support, and although I had shown my manuscript to a couple of my women "croppie" friends who had given me good feedback, I still felt like I needed the opinion of a man who was involved with the Crop Circles. So I was guided to give the manuscript to Ian Christopher, who had supplied me with a great quote to use in a magazine article the previous year. When I didn't hear back from him for a few days, I wasn't sure what to think. Maybe he was disappointed, and didn't want to tell me! When I did hear back from him, it was so incredible; I could hardly believe it (again!).

Ian makes beautiful, very meditative Crop Circle videos, put

BISHOPS CANNINGS, WILTSHIRE – JUNE 27, 2000

This photograph was taken by Phil (with my camera) from atop a Southern Electricity Board truck's cherry picker on a day of high adventure.

together from Peter Sorensen's great footage. Magically, *Crop Circle Wisdom* turned out to be exactly what he had envisioned for his next project – something based on people's personal experiences with crop circle wisdom, and the interaction of the intelligence behind them. He had no idea where he would find such a thing, and here it had landed right in his lap! Consequently, he said he'd like to use it as a central theme for this year's 2000 Crop Circle video, and asked me if he could possibly take passages from the book to use as commentary interspersed throughout the video. Both of us were absolutely delighted!

The CircleMakers' energy is coming through to us in many ways. It appears that they can even transmit their energies through the words in this book! More than one heart-centered mystical experience has occurred from someone just reading the manuscript! So, I hope that each and every one of you reading this has a truly magical experience.

I feel so blessed to be the CircleMakers' messenger; my life is so full of joy and inspiration because of it. Synchronicities continue to abound, and the blessings continue to flow.

So, a heartfelt "thank you" to everyone who has helped me with this project, particularly Linda and the team at SpiritPassage; Jak, John L., Melanie, Peter, Ron, Pete, Judy, and Ian.

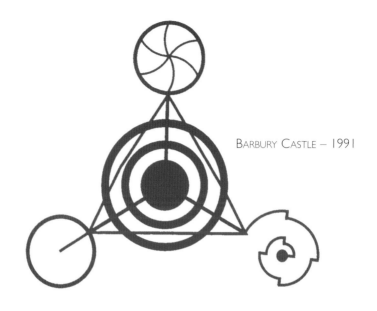

BARBURY CASTLE – 1991

The following drawings – a few of my favorite and most momentous formations from the mid to late 90's – are courtesy of Peter Sorenson, who composed them on his laptop computer from photographic images. Peter has been videotaping Crop Circles for eight years, and has documented a vast amount of formations both with aerial footage and close up interior shots.

Visit his website at:
http://cropcircleconnector.com/Sorensen/Petersorensen99.html

As we gaze dreamily beyond

STONEHENGE – 1997

DADFORD – 1998

BECKHAMPTON – 1997

BECKHAMPTON – 1998

AVEBURY TRUSLOE – 1998

DEVIL'S DEN – 1999

the stars to distant galaxies

Bythorn – 1993

or wander mysterious paths

MILK HILL – 1997

LIDDINGTON CASTLE – 1996

STONEHENGE – 1996

HACKPEN HILL – 1997

SILBURY HILL – 1997

HACKPEN HILL – 1998

ALTON BARNES – 1996

upon the sweet earth herself,

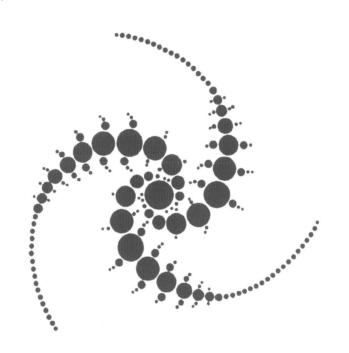

WINDMILL HILL – 1996

we realize that these flowers

Clanfield — 1998

Etchilhampton — 1997   Avebury Sanctuary — 1998

Froxfield — 1995

Littlebury Green — 1996   Goodworth Clatford — 1996

in our cosmic garden

AVEBURY — 1994

are more than mere reminders

ALTON PRIORS – 1997

EAST MEON – 1995   LONGWOOD WARREN – 1995

LOCKERIDGE – 1998

LIDDINGTON CASTLE – 1996   WEST STOWELL – 1995

of our divine connection

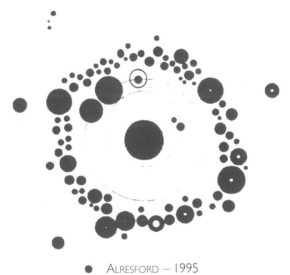

ALRESFORD – 1995

to the magnificent Universe

"THE UNIVERSE
REARRANGES ITSELF
TO ACCOMMODATE
YOUR PiCTURE OF
REALITY."

– The Superconscious Technique

Resources for Further Crop Circle Investigation

Some of the more recent books on the subject are:
Vital Signs, by Andy Thomas
Crop Circles – the Greatest Mystery, by Lucy Pringle
Crop Circles, by Michael Glickman
The Secret History of Crop Circles, by Terry Wilson
The Cosmic Connection, by Michael Hesseman

Websites:
cropcircleconnector.com
paradigmshift.com
cropcircles.org
cropcircleradius.com
earthfiles.com
cropcircleresearch.com
cropcirclespirit.com
bltresearch.com

SpiritPassage
Publishing & Communications

"*Committed to furthering body, mind, spirit, and soul communications through Spirit Consciousness*"

SpiritPassage is a New Thought ministry and non-profit corporation dedicated to the integration of Soul development and Soul expression in daily life. SpiritPassage was conceived out of the desire to be of service to others in providing a vehicle for literary and communications works, created through Spirit Consciousness, to reach others. In so doing, we firmly believe that or primary role is to serve as a vehicle or a "passageway" through which Spirit-based cosmic transmissions, modern day prophecies, and esoteric/metaphysical mystery school material, as well as integrative body, mind, spirit, and soul messages can reach the audience for which they are intended.

Through a mindfulness of watching and waiting for signs of Spirit to align the circumstances, timing, and people together for such a concept and company to be brought forward and become manifest in furthering Spirit Consciousness at the group level, SpiritPassage was born from the theory of "build it and they will come" – in drawing together others of like consciousness for the Greater Good. It is through this promise that we are gathered.

The SpiritPassage Publishing & Communications Division is committed to being of service to others by providing full-service publishing and production services to those individuals and organizations who have a message they feel led to share with the rest of the world or their community. All material submitted is reviewed with a reverence for Spirit and Truth, and all relationships associated with SpiritPassage are intended to be of the highest honor, integrity, and quality for the Highest Good of All Concerned. We are open to all submissions that fit the above mission, and offer full-service author programs as well as selected publishing services; and provide print-on-demand volume copies for limited distribution or traditional press run quantities.

As a non-profit ministry, SpiritPassage supports the practice of tithing in recognition of the universal creative energy that flows through the process of giving and receiving, and in setting into motion the "circle of return" for like measure to self and others. In like fashion, we honor and respect those individuals and organizations that are able to assist our efforts in carrying forward and expanding the ministry of SpiritPassage. Through love offerings, tithes, gifts, and grants, we are able to subsidize our publishing and ministerial efforts, and provide aid to those authors who need assistance in getting their message to their intended audience. We welcome your interest, participation, and support. Thank you.

For further information, love offerings, manuscript submissions, catalog requests, or book orders, contact:

SpiritPassage Publishing & Communications
50 Agua Viviendo
Santa Fe, NM 87505
phone/fax: (505) 466-6520
e-mail: mail@SpiritPassage.org
web-site: www.SpiritPassage.org

organizations that are able to assist our efforts in carrying forward and expanding the ministry of SpiritPassage. Through love offerings, tithes, gifts, and grants, we are able to subsidize our publishing and ministerial efforts, and provide aid to those authors who need assistance in getting their message to their intended audience. We welcome your interest, participation, and support. Thank you.

For further information, love offerings, manuscript submissions, catalog requests, or book orders, contact:

SpiritPassage Publishing & Communications
50 Agua Viviendo
Santa Fe, NM 87505
phone/fax: (505) 466-6520
e-mail: mail@SpiritPassage.org
web-site: www.SpiritPassage.org